MY HORSE
for a
KINGDOM

Living the Dream
Then Amazingly Ambushed by God

by
Elizabeth J. New

Copyright © 2016 Elizabeth New

Published in 2016

The right of Elizabeth New to be identified as the Author of the Work has been asserted by her in accordance with the Copyright, Designs and Patents Act 1988.

All rights reserved. No part of this publication may be reproduced, stored in a retrieval system or transmitted, in any form or by any means, without the prior written permission of the publisher, nor be otherwise circulated in any form of binding or cover other than that in which it is published and without a similar condition being imposed on the subsequent purchaser.

Some of the names of places and people in this book have been changed in order to preserve anonymity where appropriate.

Scripture quotations marked 'NIV' are taken from The Holy Bible, New International Version (Anglicised edition). Copyright © 1976, 1984, 2011 by Biblica (formerly International Bible Society). Used by permission of Hodder & Stoughton Publishers, an Hachette UK company. All rights reserved.

British Library Cataloguing in Publication Data

A record for this book is available from the British Library

Published for Elizabeth New by Verité CM Ltd

ISBN: 978-1-910719-39-8

Cover design and typesetting by Verité CM Ltd

Print management by Verité CM Ltd

www.veritecm.com

Printed in England

DEDICATION

To my dear friend Beth, who has encouraged me all the way, and to Sue, my ever patient sister in Christ who embraced my vision and tirelessly helped me in putting this story across. Without your help I would have failed to clear the first few hurdles let alone the huge obstacles that arose.

I love you both.

To my dearest husband Dick, who struggled to understand the circumstances of the changes in my life. That which had been so difficult for me to convey in the spoken word has at last been more fully revealed in the written word. Thank you so much for helping me on this journey where we have both laid our lives bare. You have always been my dependable, forgiving and faithful rock.

To our lovely children – you are very precious to us.

CONTENTS

Foreward 7
Preface 9
Chapter 1: THE PROMISE 13
Chapter 2: EARLY YEARS 15
Chapter 3: MALLAM 23
Chapter 4: EASTERGATE 27
Chapter 5: KAY 33
Chapter 6: PECULIAR POTIONS 35
Chapter 7: KAY SURPRISES ME 37
Chapter 8: BACK AT THE FARM 39
Chapter 9: THE MYSTERY DEEPENS 41
Chapter 10: LIFE CHANGER 43
Chapter 11: TRUTH DAWNS 47
Chapter 12: STEPS 51
Chapter 13: CHURCH 53
Chapter 14: THE CRUNCH 57
Chapter 15: REVELATION & SEARCHING FOR ANSWERS .. 59
Chapter 16: MORE STEPS 63
Chapter 17: TOM 67
Chapter 18: THE BIRTH 71
Chapter 19: LIFE AFTER 79
Chapter 20: FRESH START 83
Reflections of my Heart 89

I have seen You in the sanctuary
And beheld Your power and Your glory.
Because Your love is better than life
My lips will glorify You.
I will praise You as long as I live,
And in Your name I will lift up my hands.
I will be satisfied as with the richest of foods;
With singing lips my mouth will praise You.
On my bed I remember You;
I think of You through the watches of the night.
Because You are my help,
I sing in the shadow of Your wings.
I cling to You;
Your right hand upholds me.
Psalm 63:2–8

FOREWORD

She's done it! My amazing wife has at last committed to paper the story of her life and, in particular, the events surrounding her transformation from a person 'living the dream' to a person who has a vision to live for.

Although she has found the act of writing a struggle, her main objective throughout this process has been to be honest, and as I have read each re-working of the text, this has shone through.

I lived these events alongside her, and although I didn't understand what was happening all those years ago, and confess to only having a slightly greater insight now, there can be no doubt that her life, and the lives of those of us around her, was and is changed forever.

When these events initially happened I was angry and somewhat confused. I felt as if my wife was being taken from me, and although she went to great lengths to assure me that this was not the case (indeed she believed that our lives would be immeasurably better), it took me a long time to reconcile myself to her transformation and see that, despite the enormous change in her, she was still my Liz, the beautiful woman I married, and I was able to move cautiously from a stance of opposition to one of support for her and her new direction in life.

True to her word, we survived the initial difficulties and life has continued to be a wonderful adventure. Better than it might have been? I can't say, but it was no bad thing that her obsession with horses was replaced with a much more enquiring and open attitude to the world around her which has, in turn, enriched the lives of all those close to her, including mine.

Read her story. Trust it. For I can verify its truth in so far as I was witness to the events described. Make of it what you will, but don't dismiss it. One of my late father's favourite expressions was 'There's more to heaven and earth than meets the eye' and, who knows, there may just be!

Dick New, 2016

PREFACE

You may wonder why am I writing this account and why now.

Firstly, I owe it to God to recall this story.

Secondly, I owe it to you, whoever you are, whether you have experienced an encounter with God or not.

The Bible says, 'My people are destroyed from lack of knowledge' (Hosea 4:6). I believe it is His wish that we would all know Him and claim to be His people.

I urge you to read on with an open heart, so that you will never be able to say, when eventually the sands of time run out on you, I never knew that God loved me so much and wanted me to find Him.

As the years roll by, my growing aches and pains come as a reminder of our mortality. I seem to go to more funerals than weddings nowadays, and become increasingly concerned about the final destination of these souls.

For those who have sought and found Him, who of us doesn't hanker back to the moment of dawning that God is real? The incredible wonder, the awesomeness, the humbling, it shocks our minds and melts our hearts, and inexpressible love for Him floods in.

The Book of Revelation tells us that God is sad when His followers lose their first love and take Him for granted. Unwilling to cause Him any sadness, this statement has stirred my heart to seek the refreshing of my friendship with Him.

This book is also a journey back, for me to recall and savour that time of re-birth. I have felt a pressing need in my heart for many years to write this account.

The reason I have been able to remember so many details is because I wrote a potted version of what happened within a year of 'the happenings'. It lay hidden in a dusty drawer for nearly thirty years, until last year when I was having a clear out and was burning papers on the bonfire. It was with horror that I recognised my precious handwritten account. As the flames licked around its pages, a handy pitchfork was put to use in its rescue. I certainly hadn't intended to destroy it. Its loss would have made the telling of this story so much more difficult. This incident seemed to me to be a nudge from God that it was a story that had value and that He wanted to use. As I proceeded to write I was delighted when small and long-forgotten details dropped back into my memory.

Have you ever found that when there is something that you feel God wants you to do which seems way out of your comfort zone, you can suddenly think of so many other trivial jobs that you prefer to put first? As I battled against my inadequacy at starting this venture I became an expert in procrastination. There were so many reasons to abandon this project. I'd never written a book before, let alone getting one published. However, I have put my trust in God to see me over the many forthcoming hurdles.

I have been asked to tell this story on various occasions, mostly in Christian circles. It's called a testimony – not a particularly familiar word; it reminds me of court proceedings but in this case it signifies that I am testifying to the validity of God. Previously, for simplicity's sake I kept to the spiritual element of the story because the whole earthly story that ran beside it would seem too improbable for most people to believe. In this book I endeavour to give the full account.

If you are familiar with the Lord's Prayer you will know there is a line in it which says 'On Earth as it is in Heaven'. God was demonstrating to me on Earth what was happening to me in the spiritual world so that I would, as the story unfolded, eventually be aware of the vital part Jesus had to play in my re-birth.

I have a friend who also had a profound conversion experience. She came alongside me all those years ago at just the right time to help me understand the significant changes happening in my life. She had also written her testimony, and when I explained to her the burden I felt to do the same she encouraged me with some valuable advice: 'Just write, the words will come.' This statement gave me the freedom to get going, not to be overly bound by sentence planning, correct phraseology or worry about whether what I have written is witty, compelling or popular; that would all be tidied up later, she explained.

It's not my plan to impress you or to curry any self importance with this story, but to let God impress you with His timeless and creative plans to go after His 'lost sheep'.

I continually asked God to guide me as I wrote and, indeed, as I started the first page I felt His words to me were, 'I will help you.'

Dear reader, I have constantly felt uncomfortable about writing the 'I' and 'me' words in this story; it seems almost egotistical. But we are all 'I's and 'me's and this story could have been yours.

MY HORSE FOR A KINGDOM

CHAPTER 1

THE PROMISE

Cassie quietly pulled the cart along a country lane. Our two young daughters on board were happily chattering away to me as I walked behind, reins in hand.

Then CRASH!

Everything spiralled out of control! Like a slow-motion film switched to fast forward, this tranquil picture span around so quickly it became a terrifying blur!

One of the cart wheels had hit a deep pothole causing Cassie alarm. He leapt forward. I quickly pulled him up but, in the process, the cart and harness bumped into his rear. Shocked, he jumped forward again, causing the bumping action to repeat and, panicking, he gathered speed. He was soon galloping, going much faster than I could keep up with. I was stunned by his strength.

By now the children were terrified and shrieking. Charlotte, aged four, fell off into the side of the lane. Staggering to her feet she ran distraught after me. Vicky, still only two, had been harnessed in the cart as she was always such a fidget. Now she was screaming, adding to the noise of the clattering cart and increasing the pony's panic yet more.

At this point I was at full running speed, unable to get any traction by which to attempt to pull the pony up.

The scene resembled a Wild West film in which the galloping horses have come adrift from the stagecoach. The desperate driver, left holding the reins and being dragged at breakneck speed, body and legs out flat behind, leaving a trail of dust as the horses career across the prairie!

Just a hundred yards ahead lay the T-junction onto the main southern trunk road. I could see huge lorries flashing past.

I had no choice! I had to make the agonising decision to let go!

How could I be so stupid! In absolute terror I watched my precious daughter being galloped towards certain death.

For the first time in my life I bargained with God. 'Please save Vicky's life. I promise, in return, I will serve and follow you!'

Opposite the main road junction was the local grocery store which had a pull-in for cars. Cassie knew that a sharp right-hand turn would take him home. He tried to complete the manoeuvre at high speed and failed. The pony, cart and child all violently turned over together in an almighty crash.

With cold fear gripping every fibre of me, I ran towards the junction. I could see the pony, unscathed and by now on his feet, being held by a bewildered shop customer. Another lady had scooped Vicky up and was comforting her. She was unhurt but badly shaken. Oh, what a relief!

I felt ashamed to have risked my children's lives in such a foolhardy venture.

A miracle had been asked for and granted, and a promise had been made to God.

But my promise was soon forgotten. My passion for horses was far too strong. It eclipsed even my husband and family. I loved my colourful shiny rosettes – the symbols of my success – more. I hung them in strings around the house, often stroking and admiring them. I had dreams of winning beautiful silver cups and riding over huge show-jumping courses.

Faust, my treasured competition horse, was a striking fifteen-hand bright chestnut gelding. He was much more important to me than a rash pledge made for my daughter's life.

CHAPTER 2

EARLY YEARS

Like many young girls I had loved ponies and longed to learn to ride, but my parents were very un-horsey. Nevertheless, my wishes were granted when I was allowed to start lessons on my ninth birthday. I was hooked. From dawn to dusk I helped out at the local stables. My sister Sue and I went on to spend all our teenage years there 'living and breathing horses'. Our parents hardly saw us, except for rushed meals and bedtime.

After leaving school I attended an agricultural college and trained to be a farm secretary. I put this training to the test when I was employed as a live-in 'girl Friday' at a nearby farm. An added attraction to the job was that the lady of the house owned a horse, a large hunter called Jazz that she allowed me to ride. These people were well off; they had a beautiful house, a swimming pool and about a hundred acres of farmland. It was the first time I had moved away from home. I had my own annex in which to live and the princely sum of eight pounds a week in wages.

At the time I had a boyfriend called George. We had been in the same class at primary school together, but had lost touch for a few years once we went into secondary education. Where one went for secondary education at that time depended on the results of the Eleven-plus exam; success meant grammar school and a rosy future, whereas failure could mean a limited career path. I was the only one in my family of four children to fail. My parents were unimpressed with the local secondary modern school, which had a poor reputation, so I was sent to a private convent school where I had longer holidays than my siblings and thrived. George was the funniest person I'd ever known. He always made me laugh, and he still does almost fifty years later.

Although I was working on the farm, I was able to continue my busy social life with a crowd of friends in my home village. We met every weekend at the pub and at times 'the crowd' was fifteen to twenty strong. It was a time of gate-crashing parties, dashing around in a cavalcade of cars, walks in the countryside and generally gathering in each other's houses. We were far too innocent to get caught up in heavy drinking or drugs, and sex was definitely off limits!

At the farm, my secretarial skills proved inadequate. After missing paying some vital bills, and denting the farmer's car, I decided it might be time to move on.

My other early employment venture was six months spent with one of my stable pals at a stud farm in Devon. The farm bred Welsh Mountain ponies. The proprietor was a jolly Army major with a twirling moustache and impeccable manners. The seaside towns of Torquay and Paignton were not too far away and we often tried out their night life, aiming to attract some handsome young men –but with no notable success.

My parents had hoped for a sensible career for me, but I would spend time scanning the situations vacant column in the *Horse and Hound* magazine looking for adventure.

'English girl grooms wanted, to join Rodeo Far West,' said the advert. This American company would be touring Europe with Cowboys and Indians and all that was needed to stage rodeo shows around the continent. That sounded very exciting and, after an interview in London, I was taken on. For a country girl I was a bit out of my depth. There were

Early Years

seven English girls and we were to join the organisation at Livorno in Italy. My parents had their reservations; my father rightly stating that he knew what American cowboys were like and he was fearful for my virtue!

By now I had acquired a new boyfriend called Dick, who was introduced into 'the crowd' by George. I took an immediate fancy to him and undertook a two-timing swap on George. Dick had a bad reputation with the ladies which was well founded, but I seemed to be outlasting my predecessors. He worked in Local Government and our relationship became a long-distance one as I went off on my travels.

The rodeo days were wild. It was a huge logistical operation to transport all that was needed to put on a successful show. There were several hundred horses, wild broncos and saddle horses as well as bulls, steers and mules. An enormous amount of equipment had to be loaded and shifted from place to place. The programme included bronc and bull riding competitions, calf roping, ladies barrel racing, Sioux Indian displays plus the traditional stagecoach holdup. It was a hugely expensive set up, and its costly ticket prices meant that it was not well supported by the Europeans.

The English grooms' job was to care for the saddle horses which were kept tethered mostly outdoors on long lines of canvas mangers. You can imagine how mucky that was, especially in bad weather. I had responsibility for the care of ten Indian ponies. My only claim to fame in the show was a part in the stagecoach hold up. I was dressed up in crinolines and dragged out of the coach by wild Indians after a crazy and dangerous chase around the arena.

We toured through Europe visiting Rome, Genoa, Turin and Zurich. We would often do a town parade before the show to attract customers, which was fun. Unfortunately, the company was running at a loss and was disbanded at Rouen in France. I dread to think what became of the animals. The grooms were well paid at forty pounds a week plus hotel living expenses. At all times we were expected to wear Western clothing and enjoyed minor celebrity status in the towns we visited. We all had eyes for our favourite cowboys who thought the grooms were fair game, and some of the girls were definitely up for extra activity!

At our last venue in Rouen the showground was bleak. The horses were housed as usual in their lines, tethered to their mangers, but at least they were under cover in a large marquee. The weather deteriorated and a raging storm came through. The high winds panicked the horses, leading to the potential danger of them ripping out the tethering lines and bringing the whole tent down. It was decided to unclip them and let them loose, a distinctly hazardous operation. Meanwhile, the cowboys tried to hold down a wildly billowing marquee. Fortunately, after a chaotic chase, the loose horses were rounded up, the sun came out, the wind dropped, and all was well.

Communication in the 1970s was nothing like it is today – no mobile phones, email or Skype, and landline calls were a rare treat. I wrote letters, especially to Dick. Although life was full of adventure and my time away was only six months, I longed to be home. My zest for travel had been satisfied. I had 'broken the mould' and proved I could take on the world, but having always lived in my home village on the South Coast, my heart yearned for home, family, friends, the South Downs and Chichester harbour.

The fun was done, my final pay received and, with only the channel to cross, I would soon be home. It felt good as I pulled in to our railway station and stepped onto home soil. I hadn't told Mum and Dad I was on my way home and, as I walked in the back door, I was overwhelmed by unexpected tears. They were so proud of me and my exploits, but hadn't realised how much I had missed them.

Over the years I have met and talked to folk who have moved house many times throughout their lives and fail to understand the bond of 'home soil'. I count myself lucky to have lived most of my life in West Sussex and never cease to feel my heart lift when I return to the beckoning South Downs and the sea. It's with an inner sigh of peace and contentment that I know 'I'm home'.

Of course, I missed Dick dreadfully. They say that absence makes the heart grow fonder and it was so. Although we were both in our early twenties, behaviour in relationships was a little more 'proper' than today. Needless to say, we were hot blooded, but we did at least have to appear to have some decorum.

Dick was unsettled, he was considering a career in teaching and, in the meantime, decided to work and live-in at a community centre in Deptford, London. In time he applied for a teacher training course at Culham College, Abingdon in Oxfordshire.

As for me, what follows a job with a Wild West rodeo? Everything else seemed mundane. After weeks at home, my parents again tried to encourage me to get a 'proper job'. But I was still horse mad and took another live-in position near Salisbury, working for a crazy, posh woman looking after her children's ponies. This was not a good move. I would never advise taking a live-in position of this kind; you can end up being an 'all hours' dogsbody. That employment didn't last long and the 'proper job' finally became inevitable.

'Hospital administration,' someone suggested, 'that's what you need to get into. Nine-to-five, regular salary, safe and respectable!'

So I was sucked in, employed by the local mental hospital. Life in this job involved endlessly treading the long, Victorian corridors between offices. These were also trodden by muttering wrecks of people, institutionalised and sealed in a time warp, with little hope and nowhere else to go. The 'sane' staff were also institutionalised and formed what seemed like a rather large, dysfunctional family unit. An employee could spend years and years in this place, gradually drowning under the huge weight of paper being pushed from desk to desk. This 'red tape' conveyor belt was needed to keep the whole burgeoning monster alive.

It was still the 1970s, so there were no computers or mobile phones; communication was mostly by snail mail. I climbed the administrative ladder, moving from Patients' Affairs (curious title, but at times apt!) to Accounts, also doing some exams along the way. It was a slow death during the working day, only made bright by some good friends, social events and the creation of many inane pranks.

My relationship with Dick was in overdrive and he would come down from London at weekends. In those days one didn't live together openly, you had to have a 'plan of intent', so we got engaged. It was a pivotal point in our lives as we were both twenty-two years old and felt it was now nesting time!

We got married in my home village. The wedding took place in the same church where my parents married and my great grandparents are buried. It was just perfect; all our friends and family were there, the sun shone and our reception at an exclusive hotel was fantastic. We set off in our ancient Morris Minor car for a honeymoon in Dorset where some friends had lent us their picture-perfect thatched cottage.

We were in love; everything was rosy. We rented a flat in Benson, Oxfordshire, not too far from Culham College. Well, it was more a bedsit, one big room with a cupboard-type kitchen and an adjoining shower room. It cost the princely sum of ten pounds per week, but it was ours and it was home for almost two years.

I transferred my hospital administration job, firstly to Reading hospital, in the supplies department, then later to

Fairmile mental hospital at Wallingford. This was another Victorian asylum, similar to the one at home. Wallingford was a lovely old Thames riverside town and close to Benson. Here, I was doing payroll work. It amused me that I was able to claim tax relief for Dick as my dependant while he attended college.

We enjoyed our time there. Dick was part way through his three-year teacher training and discovering a passion for pottery. He worked hard, gaining top marks in all he did. We made good friends amongst the college students and still see some to this day. We enjoyed exploring Oxfordshire but usually raced home to Sussex at the weekends to see family and friends. Leisure time was spent sailing in the summer and walking the South Downs in the winter.

The world was at our feet. Where would we end up? After successfully completing his training, Dick started applying for jobs. In the meantime we moved in with his parents, who lived near our home city of Chichester. They were always very kind and accommodating, but inevitably we found it restricting.

Dick got a job at a school in Leigh Park, Hampshire. It was a school with a bad reputation and considered a bit of a teachers' graveyard. But he was a natural in tough situations and thrived there, teaching pottery, leading the youth club and even being drawn onto the stage where he found a haven for his big voice and extrovert personality. I had been able to make a sideways step back into the slow death of West Sussex hospital administration.

Dick's parents helped considerably in buying our first home, a small semi-detached cottage in the poorer part of a nearby village. We lived in Lower Mallam, the village being divided into upper and lower by the busy coast road. In many ways the road marked a social and economic divide.

It proved to be a great location for us, being near to the railway station. After only a few months of our move south,

I was transferred from the Chichester pay office to Worthing as a result of one of the many Health Service reorganisations, so travelling by rail was fine. Dick was equidistant in the other direction and drove to his Hampshire school.

CHAPTER 3

MALLAM

Our social life became a whirl as we were introduced into the 'Upper Mallam Set' by Jill who had grown up there. She had worked with me at the mental hospital at the start of my paper-pushing career. These people were a bit 'upper crusty' with private school backgrounds but they welcomed us into their circle, even though we were from the wrong side of the main road.

The horse world also opened up again when Jill, knowing my equine background, kindly introduced me to a local farmer and his wife who kept horses near us. Mark and Emma Hunt welcomed Dick and me with open arms. She was a young mother struggling with the stresses of family life and the day-to-day care of her horses. She readily took up my offer of help and company and we became good friends.

Mark, who was considerably older than Emma, had inherited the busy agricultural farm. He was a reserved, somewhat mercurial character, but as we got to know him our social life together grew and flourished.

Emma was of European extraction; she had an aristocratic background and I believe her family had fled the continent during the Nazi era. Although she was several years younger than me, and could be rather overpowering, I was impressed by her strong independent personality. She was an accomplished horsewoman, ambitious and confident, but also vulnerable in her need for friendship. This may have been due to the fact that she was a little isolated on the farm and her relatives were scattered. Looking back I can see how pivotal in my life this association with Emma would become.

Understanding the complicated geographical layout of this particular farm is important in the telling of this story, so I will attempt to explain. The original large, imposing, Georgian main farmhouse, formerly Mark's ancestral home, had been sold by his family in the recent past in order to raise money. It had become almost uninhabitable and needed major restoration. His family had retained the adjoining ancillary buildings and land, which Mark continued to farm, all of which now completely surrounded the relinquished farmhouse. Mark and Emma lived in what had originally been the farm workers' cottage at the start of a lengthy track, which was the shared access leading to the farmhouse, the farm buildings and the heart of the farm.

The dilapidated farmhouse had been bought by three young single men, and it was now in the process of renovation. It was their pride and joy, and a huge amount of money was being invested to transform it into three separate apartments.

We frequently socialised as one big group and became close friends with them all. Emma allowed me to ride her horses, which was both enjoyable and sometimes challenging, as I had mainly been used to riding-school animals that were usually very well behaved. Relationships between all parties seemed to be extremely happy and it was helpful to Emma to have, not only ours, but the friendship of these young farmhouse owners in her usually quiet but busy rural life.

She was an astute business woman and made extra money by buying and selling horses. She knew I was particularly taken with one of her horses, a young unbroken chestnut gelding called Faust. She offered to sell him to me but, as a newly married couple with a sizable mortgage, we had very little money to spare, and buying a horse was a huge commitment. However, Emma had an uncanny way of overcoming all my reservations and resistance and convinced me that he would be the perfect horse for me. 'Of course he can stay here with us,' she said. 'I can help you.' It was the obvious solution! Initially, to help with costs, my sister shared this commitment with me but, selfishly, I found the sharing situation challenging and negotiated an end to the arrangement.

Faust was quick to learn and before long was able to be ridden. Now my thoughts turned to his future. I had always been competitive but the dream of owning my own horse had not come to fruition until now. Here, at last, was my chance! I dreamed of winning rosettes at all the local horse shows.

Dick was generous enough to put up with this new passion in my life and even assisted me in adding a new skill for Faust by way of breaking him for driving.

Self-sufficiency had become another interest, which was fuelled by us following the exploits of 'Tom' and 'Barbara' in the TV comedy series *The Good Life*. We were now in the process of looking to buy a property with land to follow Tom and Barbara's example. We planned to keep animals and, of course, have Faust on our own doorstep.

So we found a house for sale, not too far away, at Eastergate. It was an old semi-detached house in very bad condition. However, the four-and-a-half acres that came with it were, for us, the main attraction.

There were many complications with the property; the main one being that it had what was called a 'blight order' on it. A road plan to completely demolish it formed the 'blight' and had to be rescinded before we could complete the purchase. This decision was the responsibility of the County Highways Committee; the wheels of their interminable meetings turned slowly. There was much 'red tape' to overcome in order to release the property for legal purchase and it seemed endless, but eventually we succeeded.

We had sold our previous home and, while waiting for our house at Eastergate to become habitable, we were offered a part of the unfinished renovated farmhouse at Mallam to rent. What a perfect solution!

It was a fun time. The year was 1977, the year of the Queen's Silver Jubilee. We ate and partied with our farmhouse friends, including Mark and Emma. Faust was within sight and we had bought our project home of the future.

CHAPTER 4

EASTERGATE

While renting the apartment in the farmhouse we continued with our 'day jobs', heading back in the early evenings and at weekends to the house in Eastergate to work on the incredibly wild garden. Before we could even contemplate moving in, builders were employed to take up floors, strengthen the roof, lay a damp course and inject walls. The supporting beams had serious deathwatch beetle infestations which had to be dealt with, and a new staircase was erected. All new plumbing and electrics were installed – the list seemed endless. We eventually moved in to a very incomplete shell of a house. Faust, of course, came too, and was stabled in the adjoining outhouse.

I had joined the prestigious West Sussex Riding Club and was now on the bandwagon of entering competitions. We gradually improved in show jumping and dressage and began to get good results. It was all consuming and I loved it. I had an egotistical desire to win. I would be up at the crack of dawn plaiting and grooming, cleaning and preparing all the gear necessary. There were competitions almost every weekend. It was like a merry-go-round and one that was difficult to step back from. If I did badly, I would need to prove myself again; if I did well, I had a burning desire to defend and preserve that level of success.

Alongside this, the house project steamed on with Dick and I working all hours, and builders also coming in and out. As with Tom and Barbara (of Good Life fame), our desire to become self-sufficient meant establishing a huge vegetable garden, buying-in chickens, goats for milking and pigs for fattening. As if life wasn't full enough, we decided that now might be a good time to start a family!

Our decision was based more on the pleasure we felt it would bring our parents to become grandparents, than the reality of becoming parents ourselves. The other attraction was, of course, to finally ditch the job I hated and be at home full time with Faust. These were perhaps not the noblest or most practical of reasons!

To my surprise I immediately fell pregnant, but determined that this small inconvenience was not going to change my riding ambitions or our social life. Unwisely, I continued to ride until almost my due date.

The house renovation took on a new urgency as it was hardly a habitable or hygienic environment for a new baby. The night my waters broke I had to be ceremonially carried out on a stretcher, the paramedics having to balance on planks across the upstairs floor joists because the floor was missing. Little did they know that I had been rushing around trying to tidy up the bedroom before their arrival after being told to 'lie still'.

I wasn't expecting the life-changing and emotional event that giving birth brings. The delivery was not straight forward; the baby was in a breech position and I was exhausted by the time she arrived. But how beautiful she was, how amazing. How miraculous is the perfection of a new life, an exquisite piece of humanity made, I believed, entirely by us.

Charlotte was perfect. We slotted her into our lives and carried on as before. 'This motherhood lark is a breeze,' I thought, so within a short time baby number two was incubating. We had another daughter. Now it was overload: this second baby was not quite so easy. She was more active and needed lots of attention. We called her Victoria and nicknamed her 'tricky Vicky'.

By this time we were building stables and barns, and Emma had talked me into buying another smaller horse. He was thin, generally poor and needed educating. Our plan was to build him up and sell him on. In the meantime, he was used to provide company for my precious Faust.

Faust was my pride and joy. He became well known and feared by my rivals for his achievements. The strings of rosettes grew. The fact that Dick had splashed out on a horse trailer for me meant that now the world was my oyster and I could go further afield. Faust's show-jumping success made him a real asset in riding club team events, but he often had to compete against much bigger and flashier horses. If I was going to progress up the competition ladder, I had to acknowledge that he had reached his limit. With my sights set on higher goals, and with our daughters having passed the time-consuming baby stage, how inconvenient it was to realise that I was yet again pregnant!

Regardless, I continued riding in competitions and even took a heavy fall when jumping at a prestigious show. In hindsight I was very foolish. Having been told to put my feet up, a concept I have never quite grasped, I was taken in to hospital several weeks before Sam was born. It was a joy to have a boy, not planned but so welcomed. This was definitely a family complete.

Now I had it all – I was living the dream! I had everything life had to offer: a faithful, loving husband; home and land; family, friends and horses as well. I can't say that coping with three children and all our livestock was easy, but Dick and I don't do easy! We have always been 'grafters'!

We had so much to do and so little time in which to do it! House improvements, plus building stables and barns, had to carry on after dark. Tending the enormous vegetable garden was another pressure. The added livestock also meant extra work. We had acquired, as well as chickens, two noisy goats that needed daily milking. We fattened and ate their offspring, made cheese and fed the goats' surplus milk to our pigs and puppies. We had invested in the purchase of a well-bred retriever bitch, which produced many litters. The sale of these puppies was a regular and valuable cash crop for us.

Looking back I wonder how we managed to do so much but the truth was that, although I more than pulled my weight with the daily running of our property, Dick was often left 'holding the babies' at the weekends while I was off competing.

We still maintained social connections with our Mallam friends. It was now several years since we had left to move to our own smallholding. The young men who owned the farmhouse had completed their renovations and were beginning to find themselves girlfriends and expand their business ventures. One of them had moved out and sold his part of the house. Generally, back at the farmhouse, it was a time of change.

Emma, by this time, was setting up a stud producing top-class event horses. Of course, it wasn't long before she was encouraging me again to invest in one of her growing number of livestock. We certainly couldn't afford to buy another of her horses. This latest batch commanded very high prices. Nevertheless, she had sparked my interest in breeding and, in order to help me acquire the right horse to achieve my future dreams, she suggested a plan. She had been in contact, on my behalf, with an acquaintance who desperately needed to sell a lovely but neglected thoroughbred mare and foal. To possibly breed my own foal seemed an exciting prospect, so, as if I didn't already have enough on my plate, I allowed myself to be persuaded.

We managed to negotiate a bargain price and brought Martini and her colt foal home.

The plan was to bring Martini back to top condition and mate her with Isolan, who was Emma's beautiful new black stallion. She kindly agreed to have him cover her free of charge. I was extremely grateful for this offer as his stud fee was far beyond our limited resources. Of course, the upshot of this meant that although the resulting foal would potentially be absolutely incredible, I was now heavily indebted to her.

This debt went on to become an unspoken price for my loyalty and silence in a complicated underlying unrest that had begun to emerge at the farm.

MY HORSE FOR A KINGDOM

CHAPTER 5

KAY

Kay had a mind-blowing effect on me!

'Have you met the new dentist yet?' said my mum. Kay Campbell had taken over the dental practice previously owned and run by 'Auntie Joan', a close family friend. Joan had drilled and filled my family's teeth since childhood, always rewarding us with a sixpence coin. She even let us mix the materials – which included mercury – for our fillings. Health and safety would be horrified today!

My teeth were in a pretty bad way and I was worried about what this new dentist would think and do. My mother had all her teeth taken out possibly unnecessarily and replaced with dentures soon after she was married. Apparently it was quite a common practise. I certainly didn't want the same thing for myself!

Miss Campbell was like a new broom (or toothbrush) in the dental world. She was young, attractive and in her mid-twenties. Her voice had a soft Scottish lilt which I found strangely calming.

After examining my teeth, she decided I needed some drastic dentistry. She explained that 'crowns' were on special offer at that time and I needed more crowns than the Queen! The treatment began and countless appointments were booked. Curiously, I began to look forward to my appointments and was strangely drawn to this softly spoken girl.

She said she had done some horse riding in the past so I invited her over to show off my home, my family, my horses and the Sussex Downs. Having my own horses and being able to take friends out riding meant I was a popular person to know. In my horse-orientated world, I was used to being the centre of attention. This was my domain.

'I' was the person people wanted to gravitate to. I was the one who had it all. I was in my prime. I was successful. I was independent and assured in my lifestyle. I was definitely doing Kay a favour.

Somehow, though, the tables seemed to be turned. I felt nervous and a little anxious about her visit and went out of my way to impress her. She arrived late and we took out the Land Rover and trailer with a couple of horses. I sacrificially let her ride my beloved Faust, my best horse. I began to find out a little about her life and background, and our rides became a regular event. I was making all the running with this relationship and didn't understand at all why I was so drawn to her. She was a different generation, a 'townie' and we really had very little in common. Kay had a confidence, a control of her life and a worldly knowledge that exceeded and outshone mine. She put me in the shade!

The first time she referred to her faith I was genuinely shocked. I'd never met anyone before who, to my knowledge, seriously considered the existence of God. I was taken aback and confused because my plan had been to draw her into my social life, on my terms and with my rules, but she wasn't conforming and 'falling into line'.

CHAPTER 6

PECULIAR POTIONS

It had been springtime when Martini and her foal arrived. They were in a sad state of neglect. Their previous owner, due to marriage difficulties had, in desperation, left them out at grass to the mercy of the winter weather. Thoroughbred horses are delicate, fine-coated animals that need five-star food and accommodation which, fortunately for them, was now on hand.

Martini quickly recovered from a nasty skin condition, put on weight and now, looking sleek and shiny, was transformed. The foal, which was a little small for my competition purposes, was weaned and sold on a year later. When Martini came 'in season' she was transported over to Mallam and duly mated with Emma's stunning stallion, Isolan.

I was very excited when Martini was declared 'in foal' and looked forward to the arrival of my future top-class competition horse.

Around about the time when Kay had started riding with me, Martini's health once again began to deteriorate. She was now half way through her pregnancy, but had become listless. She was not eating well and seemed distinctly off colour. Our vet was concerned. He was of the opinion that she was suffering from a heart condition and was not optimistic of successful treatment. When Emma heard my tale of woe, she suggested another possible avenue, one that appeared somewhat peculiar!

It seemed that Emma had in the past dabbled in the use of various alternative therapies and knew 'just the right person' to contact. She had grown up with 'these beliefs', she explained, and felt she may have inherited some psychic insight. 'At times I am aware I have a spirit on my shoulder,' she told me. My mental response was a picture of a colourful pirate complete with perching parrot! 'I can ask it anything. I sometimes see and sense bad future events,' she continued. 'I even believe I have seen dead people under the ground in graveyards.' In my mind I warily filed this information away, but was persuaded, as I had nothing to lose, to humour Emma and follow up on her suggestion of an alternative therapy.

Expecting a personal visit, I was a little taken aback when the healer I rang asked me to clip a piece of Martini's mane and post it to her for analysis. How and what was analysed I have no idea! I imagined someone staring into a crystal ball or stirring the hair into a bubbling cauldron. This form of alternative treatment was alien to me as I had only ever dealt with conventional medicine. My mother had warned me in my youth about things of the 'other side' after discovering that my friends and I were experimenting with a Ouija board. Consequently I was a little guarded concerning this apparent remedy.

However, a parcel of mysterious powders and tablets eventually arrived and, when administered, seemed to do the trick. Martini recovered.

CHAPTER 7

KAY SURPRISES ME

Kay had kindly invited Dick and me to a Christmas party at her house. I casually mentioned that we had accepted a couple of prior invitations for the same evening, intending to make known to her our social popularity. However, once again the tables were turned.

We arrived expecting a small formal gathering at her modest terraced house in Chichester. The reality was the opposite. We arrived fashionably late at almost eleven o'clock to find the house was crammed. Every room, and even the stairs, were overflowing with loud, raucous, trendy young people. I wasn't used to parties like this. Some of them looked like real hippy types. They were a happy, sociable lot and tried hard to make us feel welcome. Even so, I was confused. I thought I was beginning to get to know Kay, but somehow this setting didn't fit my mental picture of her at all. She obviously had a lot more going on in her life than I'd given her credit for.

Our horse-riding outings continued. Barriers began to come down and conversations turned to deeper topics. During one such occasion, as we rode along the beach, we discussed the subject of death. I can remember stating that if I died tomorrow then I was thankful to have had a very fortunate life, and would have no regrets. I didn't consider there was any afterlife and the concept of God sitting up on a cloud somewhere overseeing the world seemed completely daft. Nevertheless, she seemed to have a different opinion and offered to leave me some religious books to read if I was interested. At that time I couldn't think of anything that was less appealing!

When the books arrived I hid them from Dick; I didn't want him to think I'd got involved with some religious 'loony'. I only agreed to read them to form some common ground with her.

Both his and my parents appeared to have rejected the existence of God, and rarely attended church, although my mother had, in her youth, been a church chorister and attended in her later years. Dick's father, although absolutely the most straight and honest man you could wish to meet, had experienced the horrors of the Second World War and seemed to have lost hope in a real loving God. Both Dick and I had gone through the usual formality of infant baptism and confirmation ceremonies but they had not proved to be particularly meaningful events for either of us.

I continued to invite Kay to ride and even encouraged her to ride Faust at a show-jumping competition. This was another of my attempts to draw her into my competitive world; allowing her to compete on my precious horse was a rare privilege. However, she continued to be unimpressed and would often either arrive late or change arrangements which left me deflated. I wasn't used to being messed around!

CHAPTER 8

BACK AT THE FARM

For the farmhouse owners, the renovation and general struggling business costs had reached a critical level. Added to these money pressures, changing lifestyles meant that, reluctantly, selling their beloved farmhouse became inevitable. The property and its grounds had been beautifully and painstakingly restored to the highest level. It was now worth a considerable amount of money.

It can be viewed as understandable, perhaps, that this likely sale may have been the only possible opportunity for Mark to consider buying back the farmhouse and re-establishing the complete farm estate that he had known in his youth, but, it was apparent from the outset that it was way out of his price range. Early discussions on a possible price came woefully short of any agreement.

However, the growing need to sell was equally matched by Mark's growing desire to buy. This tension compromised the previous good friendship and relationships became strained.

In order to drive down the desirability and price of the property, Mark resorted to certain depreciating tactics. This included emphasising the worst aspects of the adjacent farmyard activity. This was partially achieved by, amongst other methods, loud machinery noises, smells, awkwardly parked agricultural equipment and threatened light industry.

We continued to socialise with both parties and were aware of the growing unrest between them. My closer association with Emma meant that she shared her feelings with me concerning the latest twists and turns in the farmhouse saga. I was of course enormously grateful to her for guiding me back into the horse world, and I was still very much in awe of her powerful personality and achievements but now, more than all of this, the free gift of my prized unborn foal had become unintentional payment for my silence and loyalty. Dick and I found ourselves unwitting 'piggies in the middle' in this situation.

It seemed to us that we had become a convenient channel for the exchange of the latest information on the progress of the sale. The farmhouse owners were incensed by the dirty-tricks campaign which was compromising their chances of selling. It made them more determined than ever not to sell to Mark. Emma eventually let slip to me that a buyer had been found and hinted at their own involvement. The truth was that Mark had got a third party to negotiate for him, keeping Robert and the other owners unaware that he was manoeuvring his way to becoming the new owner.

This knowledge put me and Dick in a truly uncomfortable position.

CHAPTER 9

THE MYSTERY DEEPENS

I continued to pursue my friendship with Kay and found ways to maintain the connection. I picked up 'those books' and made a start on *Divine Conquest* by an author called A. W. Tozer, but found it baffling; I didn't understand any of it! What was all this Spirit stuff? There were chapters on the fire of the Spirit and the power of the Spirit and many other spiritual references.

I made myself read a few pages each night in bed, before invariably falling asleep. Why did I persevere with it? It was only a small book but, for Kay's sake, I wanted to read it. I noticed that a previous reader had underlined various parts so, in frustration, I took the liberty of doing the same. I planned to debate and argue these points with her. So it continued night after night as my frustration grew.

In the meantime Kay invited us to another of her parties. Once again I was out of my comfort zone and doubted that we would know anyone else who was there. Curiously, though, as before, we were warmly welcomed. This seemed to be the same large group of people who had been at the previous party. They were kind and intensely interested in us! We noticed that they seemed to hug each other a lot, which made us feel a little uncomfortable as we were not used to this kind of demonstrative behaviour.

Kay's house mate, Clare, spent time chatting to me, along with a rather bohemian looking girl called Lydia. She said she would 'really like to get to know me', which put me on my guard. It seemed a weird thing to say. Clare at one point commented, 'Haven't you got a need for something more in life?'

'What a cheek!' I thought. Didn't she know she was talking to someone who had everything life had to offer? At least, everything I had ever aspired to. What else could I possibly want? Kay and her friends were definitely a mystery to me.

CHAPTER 10

LIFE CHANGER

It was 15 February 1987, my thirty-seventh birthday. I was snuggled up in bed while Dick was downstairs asleep in front of the television.

I picked up the Tozer book again and, with my usual exasperation, began to read. As I reached a paragraph in which he talked about 'basking in the love of God', I imagined myself basking, floating, as if in a warm sea. I was intrigued by this notion and in a moment of capitulation I addressed this God, asking, 'Are You really there? If so, then please could You show me what this love feels like?'

What was I expecting as I was asking for this 'basking' experience? Who was I asking? My expectation, in reality, was a big fat zero!

But, from nowhere, my attention was caught by the impression of a very soft buzzing, pulsating energy in the room. The light intensity grew strangely bright, then dim, then bright again. It wasn't startling in such a way as to make me afraid. Indeed, I felt a strange sort of comfort, put down the book, turned off the light and went to sleep.

I could not have foreseen what would happen in the following days and weeks.

I woke the next day, full of energy and in an unusually light and happy mood. As I drove alone into Chichester on that sunny morning I had a strange sense of not being alone, of someone or something being with me. Fleetingly, I recalled the 'parrot' spirit on Emma's shoulder but dismissed this thought. My 'someone' seemed to be filling me with warmth and pleasure, quite different from her 'spooky' description.

This was really weird! As the day wore on I began to imagine, or perhaps realise, that I now had someone to talk to. A companion who lit up my heart and made it leap, like those first-love feelings I'd had for Dick all those years ago. This 'someone' or 'something' with me knew exactly where I was, exactly what I was doing and exactly what I needed. He, or it, had my timetable in His hands. If I needed to receive an important phone call, the phone would ring as I stepped over the threshold (no mobile phones then!). When I was out driving the car, traffic lights always seemed to be green and railway gates open. Nothing slowed or hindered me. My life seemed to run like clockwork.

This visitation continued day after day and grew in intensity. It seemed as if I was living in an altered dimension. I can only describe it as somehow being on two levels: being part of my usual world but accompanied and viewing it from a distance. At times I felt enveloped within this beautiful entity, which I loved, and found myself beginning to crave and rely on its presence.

My energy knew no bounds. I started listening to music that made me want to dance for joy. Kay had lent me some cassette tapes (there were no CDs around in those days), which I played endlessly. At the time I didn't take on board that it was Christian music expressing praise to God, with lyrics that I have since come to understand.

This change and unexplained 'something' in me was puzzling. I believed it was somehow indirectly connected to Kay, although I hadn't had much recent contact with her. Was it that I sensed this entity in her and that is what had originally drawn me to her? I still had not had a chance to debate with her the underlined passages in the Tozer book. Did the book have any answers? Or maybe she could shed some light on this strange phenomenon?

I viewed the whole Earth afresh: how beautiful it was, how green the grass, blue the sky, flowers so delicate, my children, my husband and home so perfect. It was as if I had in the past viewed the world like an old black-and-white TV and now I had vibrant colour! The drab 2D world had been transformed into radiant 3D!

I remember sitting on the sawdust in a stable with this great lump of love in my heart, thinking and asking, 'Why? Why do I feel like this?' Then, temporarily it would disappear to be overcome by the busyness of the day. When this happened, and the delicious physical sensation seemed to depart, I would feel bereft and panicky. My heart would cry out, 'Don't go, please come back,' and it would – thump! It would hit my heart beautifully. Such relief! 'Who are you?' I would ask. 'What is happening to me?'

I don't know when I first called this 'thing' God or Father, but at about this time I considered going to a church, although I doubted that my 'someone' corresponded with that dry, lifeless and dusty environment. Would 'He' be there? The two seemed incongruous. What I had found was so precious, so unexpected and inexplicable that I didn't want to risk being disappointed by not finding His presence in a conventional church.

So instead I rode Faust in the beauty of the Downs, singing and loving the world, wondering if I was going bonkers! My heart was full to overflowing.

I couldn't tell Dick or anyone else what was happening to me. How would I put these things into words? He would doubt my sanity. I wasn't going to risk sharing my joy with anyone only to have them burst my beautiful bubble.

How long had that Bible been on the bookshelf? Had I even seen it before? Somehow I was drawn to it. I took it down off the shelf – it felt good. I certainly wasn't familiar with its layout at all, but if my new 'friend' was the God of this Bible, and He knew all about me, then He could certainly direct me in His book. I opened it randomly, and my eyes were drawn to some of the verses. I began to read: '[He] called you out of darkness into His wonderful light' (1 Peter 2:9). Another was, 'If anyone is in Christ, the new creation has come: the old has gone, the new is here!' (2 Corinthians 5:17). This was absolutely no coincidence! I knew without any shadow of a doubt that this was me and it was true. Wow! How amazing, how extraordinary, how different this God was to my preconceptions.

CHAPTER 11

TRUTH DAWNS

I was desperate to talk to Kay about these recent events but feeling shy didn't know how to start.

She was due to come over and ride with me but it was a wet Friday afternoon so we just rode around the local roads. I started to tackle the subject. I told her first how wonderful I felt inside and then, choking back tears, I confessed to fearing that I might lose this apparent spiritual connection with God, my friend. She replied with the most important words I was to hear in my new found Christian life, a verse from the Bible which says, 'God has said, "Never will I leave you; never will I forsake you." So we say with confidence, "The Lord is my helper; I will not be afraid"' (Hebrews 13:5–6). She asked me if I'd seen a vision. I told her what had happened in the bedroom after reading the 'basking' paragraph in Tozer's book and how shocked I was at the awesome outcome. She was surprised and appeared very excited for me.

She went on to tell me of her own story of discovering God, which was quite different from mine. I was amazed to learn that this was how God operated; that each person has their own journey, each intimately crafted by Him.

The realisation that I had found God who actually lived in me, and the fact that when I called to Him, He replied, was mind blowing. At times my heart was full to bursting with an almost delicious hugging pain. Inside my body I felt so squeaky clean and free. I just loved everyone, everything, how could life be so good? God was here on Earth! How blind I had been; how come I hadn't known this before?

'Why now?' I contemplated the possibility that I may be about to die. The secret of the whole meaning of existence revealed as a parting gift? Maybe this was how God dealt with everyone who was approaching death? If this was so, I wasn't upset. There was no longer anything to fear. How wonderful to know the truth – it offered such peace. To have known even for a short time was satisfying enough. At this time I hadn't even considered eternity or an afterlife. When I later discovered that my destiny was to be safe in His loving presence forever and ever I was blown away!

What a relief to know there was hope for the world. Maybe it wasn't doomed to chaos. Perhaps there was a master plan! If I could find my way to God, then so could anybody.

* * * * * * * * *

Each night as I climbed into bed, I would settle blissfully into God's arms. One night I had a dream. I was transported to the back of a huge building. Multitudes of people were there with their backs to me. In the distance was a blinding light which made the people in front appear as silhouettes. They had their arms and hands raised. There was music which was heavenly, so sweet and harmonious. It was an obvious act of rapturous adoration towards this figure in the distance. I couldn't quite make out His identity in the intensely bright light. I was transfixed, but apprehensive and nervous in case these people in front would turn around and see me. I felt as if I had no right to be in this fantastic place and they would be bound to evict me.

* * * * * * * * *

My love and respect for Kay had become massive; she had helped me to find God, and my gratitude knew no bounds. When I was with her, God's presence was more tangible. For that reason I wanted to pursue her, which was probably uncomfortable for her and made me feel a little guilty. I was not convinced she comprehended how powerful this life-changing experience was for me so I toyed with the idea of gifting her Martini's forthcoming foal as a thankful gesture. Nevertheless, I knew I needed to find a way to separate this tangible God presence from Kay's personal presence. If all this was true and real, I had to have my own personal relationship with Him and not be reliant on her.

Looking back, I realise that God uses His followers and His Holy Spirit in them to attract people. I'm sure Kay also had her faith built up by seeing Him at work in my life. It may have been God's plan for me to be drawn by someone 'out of the box', someone I couldn't manipulate. That was possibly why He chose Kay, with her Scottish heritage, youth, profession and strong character. She contrasted with me in so many ways.

Here I was, half way through my life. All I had held dear had changed in priority. Most of my previous endeavour now seemed to have lost its shine. It appeared a little empty and shallow. I was now going in a different direction. I was on a new path with my God in a new kingdom.

MY HORSE FOR A KINGDOM

CHAPTER 12

STEPS

What a shock this whole revelation was! I still needed Kay to take the strain and excitement with me for the time being. I had begun to introduce her to my friends but had become aware of my possessiveness of our relationship and, ungraciously, I didn't want to share her.

Kay had met my old friend Jill, and we were travelling together in Kay's car on our way to Jill's new house on the Downs. By now I was becoming increasingly agitated with the excitement and tension of this powerful love of God inside of me. I shared these thoughts with Kay, saying I felt like a balloon fit to burst and needing to be released. I also had a thousand questions that required answers.

Kay suggested that we should stop and pray! What? I didn't know how to pray. Surely not those stilted church response prayers? That really wouldn't do!

This was probably one of the most 'out of my comfort zone' moments of my life! The ball was in my court. There was no turning back.

'OK,' I nervously agreed. So we stopped at a lay-by on top of the Downs with fabulous views all around us. Actually speaking out into the ether to an unseen entity in the presence of another person is one of the hardest things I have ever done. What was I going to say? I felt so awkward and vulnerable, like a small child. Kay helped me. 'Just repeat after me,' she said, so I gave Him my heart in real live, out-loud, stuttering words.

Whoosh! I could breathe properly again. It was like a release of doves flying up to the heavens, followed by a sense of freedom and peace in my body and mind. A huge step had been taken.

CHAPTER 13

CHURCH

Kay asked me if I would like to go to a church meeting that Sunday. Of course, I agreed. I was desperate to go although I had no idea what on earth it would be like.

We had organised a big dinner party on the Saturday night for my riding club friends, but all I could think about was the church meeting planned for the following day. My dinner guests had no idea of the unseen world that I now inhabited. I marvelled at my new birth, acknowledging that everything had changed for me. It was as if I was viewing the dinner proceedings from a different plane.

By this time Dick was beginning to think something was up. He was aware of my curious, excited behaviour and sensed my reluctance to disclose the reason. He overheard a phone conversation with Kay where I was discussing my encounter with God and, mystified, he began to ask questions. I tried to explain what had happened. He was surprised and confused. That now made two of us!

Kay arrived to take me to the church meeting and there was barely room in her car for me. The other passengers were all young, noisy people. I felt a little old and staid.

We arrived at a school hall in Bognor; I was so surprised! Where was the traditional church building? Was this a genuine church meeting at all? It was crammed with mainly young people, maybe as many as two hundred, greeting, hugging and chatting. I was introduced to some and took a seat. We were in a large assembly hall which had rows of chairs around the edge and a fairly large empty space in front of a stage. On the stage was a band setting up their instruments. The band was comprised of a keyboard player, drummer, several guitar players plus some vocalists. This was all extremely unexpected.

When the music started it seemed as if I was electrified and on fire. Those feelings of God's presence that I had previously experienced were now magnified. I could hardly breathe; my heart pounded and I couldn't decide whether to laugh or cry. The songs were beautiful. The words came up on the screen which made it easy to join in. People were exuberantly dancing with complete abandonment in the open space in front of the stage. The slower more reverent songs made them raise their hands, close their eyes and at times sing in beautiful, strange harmonies. I was mesmerised – it was heavenly and I never wanted it to end. People would go up to the microphone and were free to contribute to the meeting in various ways. Some would speak out Bible verses, some would say what God had been showing them recently, some would encourage or pray, and a leader shared some teaching from the Bible. This first meeting was a most profound experience; it was intoxicating. I was reminded of my heavenly dream of a few nights earlier when I was surrounded by light, amongst the worshipping multitudes. I felt complete and happy.

I realised that these people were my new family. I had met a few of them at Kay's parties and my instinct was to throw my arms around them. I generally wasn't in friendship groups that hugged, but the need in me was so great that I just did it anyway.

At the end of the meeting Kay and Clare prayed for me to receive the gift of the Holy Spirit. In truth I'd already received it in abundance, but as Clare laid her hand on my shoulder it seemed a great heat was coming from it into my body.

The evening ended with our car load of people going to the local pub. What an amazing crowd! Not stiff, starchy or religious in the way I'd been led to understand. Who would have thought that a church meeting would finish in a pub? Apparently this was the normal routine.

I was welcomed and included. I was not just a follower of God but, as the Bible instructed, I was now adopted into His family. I had a new Father and brothers and sisters. A whole new life was opening up before me.

* * * * * * * * *

At home, in my world of horses, I had commitments to the riding club to complete. The prospect of all that this involved seemed tawdry and had lost its usual appeal. I was part of a show-jumping team which was travelling to East Sussex on a Sunday to compete at an indoor venue. Only the winning team of this competition qualified to go on to the next level of competitions. As horse events usually took place on a Sunday, the probability of interference in future church attendance looked likely and I was determined that nothing should stand in its way. My prayer to God was, 'Could we do well but not win?' My wonderful Faust, of course, put in a clear opening round which meant I had to represent the team in a jump-off against the clock. In his usual form he flew round the jumps, clearing everything at top speed. Everyone watching expected us to win and all were surprised, except me, who was relieved to hear that we had been placed second.

Thank you, God, for answering my prayer!

MY HORSE FOR A KINGDOM

CHAPTER 14

THE CRUNCH

So many things seemed to be happening and a thousand thoughts were charging through my mind. It seemed like there was a build-up of spiritual intensity inside me, guiding me on and giving the impression there was something really pressing that I had to do.

Try as I might I couldn't shake this heavy feeling. It was only a day or so ago that I had been on such a high after the church meeting. Now my sense of God's closeness had evaporated. Why could I not connect with Him? What was at the root of this uneasy feeling?

Casting my mind back I felt it began when, unknown to Kay, I considered giving her Martini's unborn foal. Maybe in reality it was an impractical idea. Although my original plan had been to breed the ultimate show horse for myself, I felt it was important to offer Kay a precious gift in gratitude for guiding me to God. However, this potential present had in its beginnings 'strings attached'. I could not forget the fact that the circumstances of its conception revolved around the farm and Emma. I carried a sense of guilt and shame brought on by my conflicted loyalties, secrecy and seemingly two-faced behaviour concerning the sale of the farmhouse. My preference would have been to give Kay a perfect gift that was completely unconnected with all this, rather than one sullied by my deceit.

I hoped that if there was another step to take or a problem that needed solving, God would help me identify and deal with it. I hated this feeling, it was as if He had somehow become out of reach.

Unexpectedly, Robert, our closest farmhouse friend, came over to visit us at Eastergate. Our friendship with him had remained amicable despite the unpleasant situation back at the farm. He had negotiated the purchase of a new home nearby and had started the process of moving in. It seemed we were about to become neighbours.

He caught up with me when I was on my own in the stable yard and informed me that completion of the sale of the farmhouse was only two days away. Although all the necessary paperwork was almost complete, he hadn't met the new buyer and was still unaware of his or her identity.

For him to consider or suspect that this buyer, even at this eleventh hour, might be Mark using a third party to make the purchase on his behalf would, after all his years of hard work and genuine love of the place, be an extremely bitter pill to swallow.

Then, knowing my close relationship with both Mark and Emma, he asked me 'that' question: 'Do you know who has bought it? Is it Mark?'

I wanted the ground to open up and swallow me! I was caught on the spot. What was I to say? Should I tell a lie and deny knowledge? Should I 'fudge' and tell a half-truth in order to 'save face'?

Or should I 'come clean' and confess?

I knew that now I was a Christian, to tell even a small fib would cause pain both to me and my wonderful God. Things were different now. I had to be honest.

I admitted that I knew Mark was the buyer.

This was shattering news for Robert. His worst suspicions were realised.

I felt terrible.

CHAPTER 15

REVELATION AND SEARCHING FOR ANSWERS

At bedtime we had been reading the series of Narnia books by C.S. Lewis to the children. Up until now I had been blind to their deeper meaning. As I read with new insight, I realised that, like the children in the first book, *The Lion, the Witch and the Wardrobe*, I had stumbled upon a new world.

Quite by chance, our children had decided some time earlier that Martini's foal, when it arrived, should be called Aslan after the Lion in the story. This suited me as, traditionally, a well-bred foal carried a name association with its sire. In this case the father's name was Isolan, so the name Aslan was perfect.

In the story, Aslan was the children's friend and guide. In order to save the life of one of them who had been imprisoned, he offers his life in exchange for the child's freedom. It dawned on me that the author was mirroring the story of Jesus Christ. How uncanny that the very name our children had chosen represented the Son of God.

This was curious and posed questions for me.

Was God trying to tell me something?

Was it just coincidence that these thoughts were coming to me just as I was discovering God's truth or did they have greater significance?

This Jesus thing was a mystery to me. I really didn't know how He fitted in to my recent experiences.

I figured that if God was trying to speak to me, I needed to collect and reflect upon these thoughts and maybe look a little deeper into these C.S. Lewis stories. I was beginning to see that He could use anything or anybody to get my attention.

Our bedtime reading had moved on to another book in the Narnia series called *The Voyage of the Dawn Treader*. The children in the story journey in a boat to the ends of the Earth. In the final chapters, one of them must leave the boat and go off into the unknown, through surrounding mist to a promised shining destination.

Once again I found myself identifying with this story to the extent that I was becoming uneasy. Was this a reflection of my journey? Where was I going? What did it involve?

These books had been gifts from dear old Auntie Joan, the dentist. I wondered what had prompted her to give them to me. I knew she attended church regularly but was she a Christian? It took some courage to make the phone call and ask some probing questions. I was disappointed to learn that although the stories were significant to me, it was apparent they were just tales to her.

My thoughts turned to the name Faust. It occurred to me that when I first bought him he had already been named by Emma. I had never previously considered its origin. It suddenly struck me that his name also had significance. The name rang a bell. Who was Faust?

On further investigation, I discovered that Faust was a character from German legend who had sold his soul to the devil to gain knowledge, worldly riches and pleasure. I conceded that my horse-riding obsession and success in competing had definitely been the love of my life up until this point. My husband and children had been sacrificed in favour of my pursuit of success in the equestrian world. In my own way I had been seduced by a powerful worldly pleasure. Now my love and knowledge of God had won my heart and my priorities had changed. I felt guilty about letting my family and farm friends down. I had been leading a wrong and self-centred life up until this point and it was weighing heavily on my mind.

I was beginning to get the impression that God was shining a light into areas of my life that I wasn't proud of and encouraging me to take a good look at them.

I phoned Kay's dental surgery to make an appointment but really it was an excuse. I was missing her and wanted to speak to her personally. These latest revelations bothered me and I needed to talk to her about them. Was there an issue that needed resolving? Perhaps prayer would help me dispel this uncomfortable feeling? So we arranged to meet a few days later.

* * * * * * * * *

At night I would dream and settle comfortably in the heavenly place. How easy it had been to find my way; surely I could carry Dick there as well? I would lay my burning, anointed hand on his sleeping chest willing him to join me. Then I realised that it wasn't that easy. God had a different route and plan for him, and indeed for anyone else who chooses to seek Him. I sadly concluded that he and I were somehow living in slightly different dimensions and that it was God, not me, who was in charge of his destiny.

With Dick very much on my mind and aware of the presence of God, I drove to school the following afternoon for the usual daily pick up. Feeling very downhearted and needing support, I decided to 'test the waters' and approach a lady called Sue who was known to be a Christian.

I was definitely taking a risk 'blowing my cover' with her. Some of my previous probing with people had backfired, but I was hoping that she was different and had received this overpowering love of God in the same way I had.

She looked puzzled as, with tears in my eyes, I stumblingly tried to impress on her my sadness in not being able to take Dick with me into the Kingdom! She was taken aback at my words, but as I managed to explain a little more she became aware of whose Kingdom I was referring to. The 'penny dropped' and she realised I was, in my own way, trying to make sense of a profound, spiritual, life-changing event. She responded in a perfect manner. Her strong loving arms engulfed me.

What a relief! She knew God as well. Were there any other believers here at the school, I wondered?

She hugged and hugged me and, as if reading my mind, she pointed across to a different mum saying, 'She's another one! Forgetting my earlier sorrow and excited at finding true believers, I rushed over to her declaring, 'I made it! I made it!'

Her face was a picture as she also tried to work out what I was saying. Then, with hopeful apprehension, she ventured, 'Are you saying what I think you're saying?' I gleefully nodded. I saw her overcome with surprise and happiness. Then came more hugs and tears! These women understood my joy at finding soul mates and new sisters. They also expressed love, hope and comfort over my concern for Dick.

God had provided them at just the right time. Little did I realise how important this supportive and wise group of women would become over the coming years.

CHAPTER 16

MORE STEPS

I felt buoyed up by my discovery of fellow Christians and was excited to be able to tell Kay and Clare about it when we met that evening.

Without informing Dick of my change of plan, instead of going to the exercise class I would normally attend I headed over to Kay's house with a sense of urgency. I needed relief from the turmoil of thoughts and revelations that were bothering me. There was the hope that this 'off loading', particularly regarding the situation at the farm, would bring more clarity to the next step which I felt was imminent.

The area of Chichester where Kay lived was a maze of tiny streets and, although I'd been before, somehow I just couldn't locate it. I stopped at a corner shop to ask the way and bought some wine as an offering, worrying that I might be becoming a nuisance to Kay and Clare. Frustrated, at not being able to find her house, it began to occur to me that maybe something or someone was trying to prevent me from keeping this appointment.

Eventually I spotted the right road and pulled up outside her home. It was then that I could smell burning and noticed smoke billowing out from under the car bonnet. Was it going to explode? I was too scared to even turn off the engine. I leapt from the car and banged on Kay's door.

By this time the smoke was intense and I was even more convinced that there was some kind of conspiracy, a strange plan, to hamper this meeting.

When Kay opened the door and saw the smoke she was shocked and immediately called the fire brigade. I don't know how I plucked up the courage to return to the car, open the door and switch off the ignition. Within minutes the fire engine arrived with lights flashing and sirens blaring. It blocked the whole street. What a commotion for the neighbours! The firemen managed to open the bonnet and sprayed an extinguisher under it. The job was done and the fire was out.

When the commotion had died down I managed to tell them about some of the issues that were troubling me, in particular the story concerning the sale of the farm house and the uncomfortable feelings of guilt and shame over the disloyalty towards these friends. It was the first time I had fully admitted to myself that I had not been honest, and now I took responsibility and openly faced my duplicity. I had tried unsuccessfully to justify my actions but, now it was confessed, I knew it was wrong. They prayed for me, my faltering words reflecting my heart of sorrow. I gave it all to God, my new friend, and He took it away. I was released.

I had been completely unaware of how much my sin offended this Holy God and would cripple our relationship if not acted upon. Although on the scale of the world's immense wrongdoing this would rank as a trivial issue, any unconfessed sin is abhorrent and causes separation. It was vitally important that I should acknowledge this offence and ask for His forgiveness. God, true to His Word, set me free from the hold it had on me and led me back onto a clean and clear path. Thank goodness He had brought it to my attention! Now I had peace.

I knew now that nothing could stand between Him and me. I was truly forgiven and truly saved.

Kay drove me home that evening and I had to tell Dick the tragic car story. As usual, he just took the news in his stride and resolved to try to recover the car a couple of days later.

I felt cherished and secure again and, that night, while in a half sleep, I sensed God's closeness to me. It felt as if I sat at his feet and we talked endlessly. He was so loving, funny and reassuring.

Our car troubles continued over the next few days. Not only did I get stuck at the school with a flat tyre on our Land Rover, but even a borrowed car appeared to carry that unpleasantly familiar burning smell.

Dick's attempt to retrieve the stricken car in Chichester was also fraught with difficulties. Amazingly, the engine started, but soon broke down again. After huge hassles and wasted hours it was eventually towed home.

We seemed to be plagued by 'gremlins'! Was this my imagination or was the idea of a negative spiritual opposition a possibility?

MY HORSE FOR A KINGDOM

CHAPTER 17

TOM

Dick had told me sometime previously that his chiropodist was a Christian and a church elder. As he lived locally I decided it would be sensible to talk to him about my new-found faith and perhaps get some reassuring answers to my many questions.

Dick had been involved in a traffic accident when he was sixteen years old. He was one of the original Mods of Mods and Rockers fame. He had the scooter plus the more-than-necessary mirrors, the green parker and the 'attitude'. One afternoon, whilst on his way back from work, he unintentionally mounted a bank on his scooter and ended up coming off into the path of an oncoming coach. His foot was crushed under the wheel of the coach and the kick-start pedal on his scooter sliced through the main artery of his leg. He almost bled to death!

Miraculously, in the car immediately behind the coach there was a nurse who happened to have a tourniquet on board. The next car held up in the resulting traffic jam was a police car whose driver radioed for an ambulance. Dick says that he and the sole of his foot travelled separately to the hospital! His injury was serious and he had been told to prepare to have his foot amputated. Fortunately, it was discovered that a top London surgeon was staying in the area who kindly agreed to come to the hospital to operate and try to save his foot.

Although Dick was told to get used to the idea that any future career would be desk bound, the reality has been quite the opposite. He has not been held back in any way and his 'moves' on the dance floor are legendary.

There were many further operations though, some toes removed and skin grafts done. When I met him he still walked with a stick. His nickname became 'Dick the Stick' and he used to show off his many stick-balancing tricks.

The upshot of the accident meant he has needed continual chiropody treatment even to this day. The scar tissue produces corns and the skin is very fragile, but how kind of God to provide him with a Christian chiropodist, especially at a time like this when I was discovering God and needed some wise counsel.

I initially made arrangements for Tom to visit when I knew Dick would be out. I felt it was better not to present Dick with any situation where he might feel worried or excluded. He is a very down-to-earth person, so expecting him to believe in a supernatural re-birth without experiencing it personally would have been like asking him to believe in fairies.

My mind was in a whirl. Dan the decorator was painting the stairwell, overseas visitors were due and Martini's foal was imminent. Overriding all of this, though, was a disconcerting sense of unease. Although I was very much aware that the presence of God appeared to be uplifting me and that He was in control of all that was happening around me, I was also beginning to be aware of an opposing force – there was another side to the coin.

Was it coincidence that I had, that afternoon, narrowly avoided yet another car accident? Even as I went out in the early evening to check on the horses, the darkness seemed heavy and foreboding. Was there something in this troubling atmosphere that I was being shown? I was going to have to trust my God and wait and see!

My concerns increased and I didn't want to be alone while I waited for Tom to arrive so, changing my mind, I told Dick that Tom was coming. He could see I was agitated and agreed to stay with me. (He later said he wondered if I was having a mental breakdown.) 'What about Dan?' he said, 'We can't talk to Tom about this personal stuff with the decorator here.' Within minutes Dan appeared looking flushed and sweaty saying he suddenly felt unwell and was going home.

I thanked God. It was good of Him to demonstrate that once again He had everything covered.

My earlier thoughts concerning a possible enemy had multiplied in my mind. I had the impression, like a dark cloud hovering, that a significant event was coming but was unsure of its exact nature.

Tom arrived and was perturbed to find me distressed. I was relieved to see him. I felt safer. Here was a man of God! Maybe he would put my mind at rest?

Instead of addressing my unease, Tom appeared more concerned with reassuring Dick. It seemed to me that he made light of my shock discovery of God and the hidden spiritual realm. After trying to explain my concerns, I got the impression that he wasn't taking me seriously. He damped me down and made me feel foolish.

Incensed, I raised my voice, 'Look, the Kingdom of God isn't just in heaven. It's here on Earth, NOW!' This was blindingly obvious to me! His apparent dismissal of my revelation of God's Kingdom was infuriating.

He left. He must have found himself having to make the difficult decision as to which of us was in the most need! Although I didn't appreciate it at the time, He knew that

God would take the best care of me and therefore Dick became his first priority.

I went to bed upset and disillusioned. I thought Tom would add some credibility to my experiences and confirm all I had told Dick about God and His Kingdom. How could the leader of a church put me down like that? It felt like he had attempted to crush my faith and make me doubt the validity of what I had experienced.

At the children's school, the news of my freshly found Christian faith had spread, and after speaking to the original two mothers a few days earlier, that number had now grown to five. This lovely group of Christian women consoled and affirmed me. I had found God! My experience was true and genuine.

Over several cups of coffee, we pored over the Scriptures which revealed the absolute supremacy of God over any darker spiritual powers. This finally allayed my fears and put my mind at rest. I had been struggling to make sense of these incidents and realised God wanted me to know that not only was I precious, loved and cared for, but He was trying to teach me that He was always my reliable safety shield.

Sue wrote me a letter pointing out scriptures from the Bible which helped me to put my salvation into perspective. I was particularly taken with one stating that all the angels in heaven celebrate when a new soul comes to God: 'There is rejoicing in the presence of the angels of God over one sinner who repents' (Luke 15:10).

I had managed to finish reading *The Voyage of the Dawn Treader* to the children and, although my heart was in my mouth all through the final chapter, the story had a peaceful and beautiful ending. The traveller that I thought might be going to his death was joyfully reunited with his King!

CHAPTER 18

THE BIRTH

Things quietened down over the next few days. My mind, however, was consumed with sweet and inexhaustible conversation with my dearest faithful God.

I was becoming aware that another spiritually significant event was looming. It was with nervous anticipation that I contemplated what on earth it could be. Why did it seem that it held monumental importance? Was it possible that it could it be connected with me personally, or even to the birth of this foal? If so, how and why?

I cast my mind back a few weeks to the time when I thought maybe God's appearance in my life was because I was about to die. Is this what He was still preparing me for, or could it be something even more epic like the heralding of the Second Coming of God? It remained a complete mystery.

As I was getting used to trusting God with my plans, instead of worrying I placed Martini's birthing situation firmly in His hands. I fully expected Him to oversee the safe delivery of her foal. I had a fanciful notion that it would be born on a Sunday, the Lord's Day – what could be more appropriate.

I woke with a start at two o'clock on a Sunday morning. Clothed in my dressing gown, I padded out into the darkness and down to the stables. It was a still, calm, mild night. Martini was restless and in a sweat. She was continually lying down and getting up, and obviously in labour. I went back to the house, got dressed and woke Dick. Armed with a foaling instruction manual we went back to the stables and started a vigil.

I had given birth to three children and it was never an easy job. They just came when they were ready, regardless of the time it took or the pain they caused. I wasn't aware that mares generally foal fairly quickly and we were now several hours into her labour. She was straining, sweating and rolling alarmingly, her distress obviously increasing.

It was fortunate for us that Robert, who was now our new neighbour, had been forgiving and hadn't disowned us over the withholding of information concerning the sale of the farmhouse. He now had a partner who had valuable stud and foaling experience. She had very kindly offered to come and help if we had any problems with the birth. Although it was a crazy time of night to wake anyone, Dick drove to rouse the sleeping couple and seek advice. Fortunately, he was able to wake them and within no time Robert's partner, despite being heavily pregnant, had without hesitation dressed and accompanied him back to our stables.

It was ascertained by internal examination that the foal was incorrectly positioned inside the mare and unable to be born. A vet was needed quickly. Fortunately, even though it was about five o'clock in the morning, we were able to contact an emergency vet and, to our relief, he arrived quickly.

Although Martini was very distressed, it was confirmed that the foal was still alive. Repositioning a foal inside its mother and attempting to pull it out is no mean feat. The normal birth position is front feet first with head and neck over the outstretched limbs. The foal was stuck with its head turned sideways. Eventually, with his arm completely inside the mare, the vet manoeuvred the foal's head into a better position. Ropes were then slipped around the protruding hooves. Dick and the vet had to use all their strength to pull him out, timing their 'pulls' with her contractions. It was very stressful and upsetting to watch.

Somehow I'd always known it would be a colt foal – it was fitting. He eventually emerged, slithering to the floor, alive and breathing, but just moments later everything changed. The vet suddenly rushed for his bag, prepared a syringe and pumped drugs into him, slapping him and blowing into his nostrils, trying to get a response.

It was no good. The trauma was too great. He died there and then. He was so beautiful and perfect. His dark brown head had a small star.

The vet was surprised and upset. He honestly thought the foal would survive. He tended to Martini who was puzzled by her dead foal lying on the ground. How sad for her. She had suffered so much.

Now I was confronted with doubts. Perhaps I should have called the vet earlier. Was I foolish to have left it so late?

We were shattered! It was six o'clock in the morning. The children would be up soon, so I collapsed into bed for an hour. Sleep did not come easily as I tossed the events of the night round and round in my head and pondered the irony of Robert's link once again appearing in this unfolding story, this time via his partner. I struggled to make some sense of what had happened.

Where was my beautiful God in all this? Surely He knew everything. Had he stood by and let this happen?

Although I had earmarked Aslan as a gift for Kay, would it actually have happened? Would I have given him away? Maybe the whole idea was a whimsical, unrealistic notion? The chances were that he would still have been my future dream horse.

Why did so much hope and potential have to end in death? Was this some sort of cruel test between my love of horses and my new-found love of God?

I had been so full of anticipation and tension over the preceding days, almost like a inflatable filled to bursting point. Now it was popped! It was deflating, the air released, hopes were dashed, the dream had died.

Although I was aware of God's presence, I needed a real heart-hugging reassurance that He was still in charge. The choice, if this is what it was, was really no contest. There was no doubt about the preferred choice in my mind. My love for horses would never be able to compete against my love for this all consuming eternal God. He was totally irresistible!

After sleeping fitfully, I woke to a beautiful, cloudless spring day. My children were up and contentedly amused. They were oblivious to the night's events and we held off giving explanations until there was a more appropriate time. As it was Sunday, the Lord's Day, I was determined to find a place where I could ask God what all these events meant and generally seek solace in His presence. I set off for the local Anglican church but, unfortunately, it was closed. Undaunted, I drove to one in the neighbouring village.

It was comforting to absolutely commit my life once again to God through the communion service and it gave me peace. As I left the church and spoke to the officiating priest, I tried to explain my presence there that morning but, sadly, I felt that my words didn't register with him.

At home poor, long-suffering Dick was digging and liming a grave for the foal, and Aslan was duly buried.

I phoned Kay to let her know what had happened. She was sympathetic but had never been aware of my wishful plan to give him to her. She seemed not to have comprehended how epic the events of the last few months had been for me, all of which seemed to culminate in the foal's death.

In the evening I went to the Revelation Church meeting and felt hurt when Kay stood up at the microphone and said what a beautiful spring day it had been. She spoke of the flowers and trees budding, all bursting into life. I thought of my dead foal that I had wanted to give to her still warm under the ground.

This whole episode of my life, since I had met Kay, had been like a journey to an unknown destination. It seemed I had been following signposts that led me onwards to various points and key places where I had to make certain discoveries. At each place information was revealed and needed acting upon. This final place, tied up with the dead foal, seemed to be the most important of all. What information was being revealed here? What was the whole picture?

As I mentally began to lay this tragedy alongside the Bible story of Jesus, certain significant thoughts registered.

For the disciples and followers of Jesus, He was the man of promise. He was the hope of freedom for the subjugated nation of Israel. He appeared to be the promised Messiah.

But hope died with Him. They were devastated.

Little did they know it was part of God's master plan. His death wasn't a tragedy but a triumph!

Through His birth, ministry, death and resurrection, He had opened a door for all men to be reunited with Him. Consequently, He held it open for me and I, too, had been ushered in.

For the first time I recognised that this doorman absolutely had to be Jesus! He was the one I hadn't encountered before. He had the key to the door! His death had made my entry into God's Kingdom possible. He was the last, and most important, piece of the puzzle. Now there was a complete picture comprised of three parts: a wonderful heavenly Father, a treasured, sacrificed Son Jesus; and the comforting, magnetic Holy Spirit. They had all worked together in loving union to bring me to this place. This was my permanent, new, loving family and my eternal home.

I was amazed at my journey! How sweet and perfect it was. What a creative, storytelling God He was. He had planned it all along. All I had to do was to step into it and walk it with Him.

He had revealed this whole process in 'bite sized' sections, like pieces of a jigsaw. To have been presented with the completed picture in one instance would have been beyond my comprehension.

I recalled school scripture lessons and things said in the past by teachers and ministers in various church services, and sadly realised how much the words telling of God's hugely important saving plan for mankind had gone straight in one ear and out of the other. It had come across to me as empty words. Perhaps it is considered by most people as just a nice comforting idea which they seem to drop as they grow older.

The basis of the story, I remembered, was that Jesus claimed to be the Saviour of the world. He took with Him our sins when He died on the cross. After three days He was resurrected to show that He overcame death and consequently death could also no longer hold us captive. Our sins were paid for – eternal life is ours for the taking.

Those words, in just a few vastly understated sentences, could never have prepared me for this fantastically amazing place to which I now had free access, and where I found its King poured out endless love and acceptance to me.

Jesus actually died for me! He did an exchange: His life for mine. Now my old life was willingly surrendered in the same way, and I was irreversibly connected to Him. I had been given a new birth, an intimate connection with Him and a fresh start. This was certainly something I didn't earn or deserve but how fortunate and grateful I was to have responded to His prompting.

This was real. I had discovered the gateway to God.

The knowledge of the Holy Spirit and Almighty Father God had come to me in a supernatural manner. In the same way that Jesus had come to earth, so the revelation of His identity to me through the horses was also earthbound.

Although it was a pale comparison, this whole earthly story, starting with the conception and finishing with the death of Aslan, was like a Bible parable, also holding a likeness to the exchange of lives made in my children's Narnia story. It had been God's way of speaking to me personally by using people, animals and events in my life to make His purpose known.

Similarly, through the birth and life of Jesus, His voluntary death on the cross and His subsequent resurrection, He paid the price for our sin and rebellion in order to bring us into the love and knowledge of Almighty God.

Comparably, Aslan's death also signified the death of my intense, futile and unimportant relationship with horses. This was no match for the contentment I now found in God. Its former grip on my life died.

The subsequent birth of Robert's beautiful daughter, who unexpectedly and by chance was given the same Christian name as me, acted as a poignant reminder of my new beginning.

I was born again. My life was regained, this time to be lived differently. To be lived as His gift to me, His life, His way, His truth.

* * * * * * * * *

Jesus replied, 'Very truly I tell you, no one can see the kingdom of God unless they are born again.' (John 3:3)

Jesus answered, 'I am the way and the truth and the life. No one comes to the Father except through Me.' (John 14:6)

For God so loved the world that He gave His one and only Son, that whoever believes in Him shall not perish but have eternal life. For God did not send His Son into the world to condemn the world, but to save the world through Him. (John 3:16–17)

CHAPTER 19

LIFE AFTER

As I write this in 2016, Dick and I continue to live at Eastergate on our smallholding. In my desire to use my life and our property for God's glory, we overcame the hurdles of necessary planning permission, licensing and teaching qualifications, in order to open a legitimate riding school. We operated successfully for fourteen years, during which time many hundreds of children and adults passed through our gates and learned to ride. Many also heard the good news of Jesus' mission on Earth and a few found their way to Him.

During this time there were countless hours of lessons, gymkhanas, holiday events, camping, South Downs riding and exhaustingly much more. There is a saying which warns about the problems encountered when working with children or animals. I took on both of those unpredictable entities at once, sometimes in large numbers, and can honestly say that the other saying, 'God gets me out of scrapes', was true and vital in the running of my establishment. Without His protection for my riders and horses I would have been lost.

It has taken many years for God to temper my competitive spirit, but it never again controlled my life. Together, Vicky and I took our various horses to many shows where we were moderately successful.

Faust lived to a ripe old age and was a favourite in the riding school. Unfortunately Martini's life came to a premature end after a serious colic attack.

My three children helped and rode in the riding school and followed me into church life, all of us being baptised and involved in ministry work. Charlotte worked for 24/7 Prayer Ministry for five years.

My church life at Revelation in Chichester continued for about ten years, after which I was involved in a church planting scheme into my local area. Since then I have spent the last eighteen years in our local village churches. I love to sing worship to God and, using my limited guitar skills, I have for many years led the worship in house groups, prayer meetings, old people's homes and various other gatherings.

Soon after my Christian conversion, Kay left this country for Australia where she continued her dental career. Unfortunately Mark and Emma's marriage foundered and they separated. Mark lived mostly alone in the farmhouse and sadly died in his fifties.

I have had an incredibly fortunate life, full of great friends and family. I am so proud of my husband and beautiful children, and thank God for their church upbringing which has no doubt helped in moulding them into fine, loving, honest people.

And now when I lie in my bed, in that same room where my Lord first rescued me, and reflect on these events, it prompts me to savour life. I taste every tiny morsel of it, chew it around and endeavour to get the maximum out of it!

As I get older I appreciate His creation even more, each spring appearing more beautiful than the last. I thank Him for those that I love and for those who love me. I say that life is good!

Dick and I are now both retired but are busier than ever with grandchildren, a few elderly horses, sailing, upkeep of our property and church commitments.

I continue to be excited, empowered and energised in my journey through life with God. I am continually amazed at the miraculous way He interacts with us, sometimes in the most unexpected of circumstances.

We are happy and healthy and very grateful to have the love and leading of the Lord.

If you are searching for answers to those big questions in life, don't give up. In the Bible Jesus also says,

Ask and it will be given to you; seek and you will find; knock and the door will be opened to you. For everyone who asks receives; the one who seeks finds; and to the one who knocks, the door will be opened. (Matthew 7:7–8)

MY HORSE FOR A KINGDOM

CHAPTER 20

FRESH START

How to conclude this last part of my story has been the most challenging. My desire for the reader is that all becomes clear, your questions are answered and the loose ends are tied up. In reality I know this is impossible; my story did not finish at this point – in actual fact it had only just begun.

When my family used to undertake a jigsaw puzzle, like many we would find all those pieces with a straight edge first in order to build the frame of the picture. Invariably the most difficult parts of the picture were the last to be completed.

I felt that God had given me this really important and life-saving framework and the many unanswered questions represented the jigsaw pieces. There were hundreds of them! I still don't know how extensive the picture is, as I continue to build the picture of God and His past and future plans for mankind.

I know and trust that as I search for answers they will be found. The Bible is an inexhaustible and inspirational source which not only traces God's covenant with man from the beginning of time, but also teaches us how to respond to any and every situation in which we find ourselves today.

Re-examining my conversion experience has been an exciting and faith-affirming exercise. I have been able to recognise a beautiful and ordered ushering into God's kingdom, and although on the surface it seemed like a series of random co-incidences in circumstances, names and situations, there had always been the hidden purpose of a final destiny.

When I recall that hasty promise made so many years ago concerning the runaway child, pony and cart, I realise that God took my plea for Vicky's life absolutely seriously. It took four years of my ignoring that promise before I heeded the call to respond to His unusual way of prompting me to find Him. When I was unfaithful to my word, He was trustworthy to His.

My impression is that God delights in our adventure and He loves to unveil the mystery. There is a sense of our being encouraged and spurred on as our once-closed minds wrestle with the supernatural, the unimaginable, the miraculous and, ultimately, the truth.

* * * * * * * * *

This picture came into my mind.

Life is like a play set on a stage except, unlike those in the world, there are no rehearsals. There's just one chance to get the production right. The Holy Bible is the script. Each player knows in their hearts the lines and actions that are appropriate for their part. However, there is a 'terrorist' in the cast whose intention is to spoil the show and steal the leading role from the appointed star. This 'terrorist' hovers in the wings, scene after scene, trying to get the players' attention and divert them from their parts. He may tempt them with notions of grandeur or disable them in some way, maybe even attempting to change the script. He will try any trick to hold up proceedings. Indeed his methods of disruption are endless. It is, therefore, a mental and physical challenge for all the players to battle through and complete the production. It eventually comes down to a choice for each member of the cast. The question posed is this: are they going to 'get this show on the road' and follow the producer's direction or will they allow themselves to be side-tracked and possibly never reach the final curtain?

* * * * * * * * *

The 'terrorist' loves to keep us busy. How many of us feel rushed and chivvied through life? From childhood, through education, the workplace, then maybe on to partners and families, the time flies by. Before we've had a chance to draw breath, old age is upon us and the opportunity to contemplate the big questions of life are rarely fully addressed.

All through the ages, great thinkers have mulled over these topics. Does God exist? Are we here by chance and born out of a cosmic explosion? Are we accountable to anyone? Is there a purpose to our lives?

Over the years I have loved hearing the conversion accounts of other Christians. They are so varied and full of twists and turns. They have ranged from the lengthy traditional building of faith through the established church to the blindingly dramatic. Whatever the route, each soul is vitally important and celebrated in heaven as they find their way.

I count myself lucky that, unusually, I found God not through experiencing trauma or desperation, as I was more than content with my worldly life, nor through normal church life, but unexpectedly and undeservingly I stumbled upon an irresistible encounter where I met with His love first hand.

The simplicity of loving God and having a true friendship with Him, all available because of Jesus' saving plan for mankind, is not the onerous rule-keeping toil that is portrayed. The delight in praising, adoring and pleasing someone who loves you is natural and easy. The provision of love, comfort, eternal security and Fatherly care that He lavishes on us is infinite.

I fell in love with the Bible when I realised it was 'His-story'. It has been divinely designed as the perfect manual for living, bringing comfort, guidance and hope for mankind. Many times the words written seem to leap off the page as if God is trying to speak to me, usually pointing out some new truth. I shudder when I look back and consider that I had dismissed it as a book of legends with no historical basis; now I know it is pure treasure. Studying the Bible has been a natural part of my life for many years, and although I realise it can be a daunting book to venture into, I encourage you to ask God to guide you if you take up the challenge to dip into it.

When God gives us a new start, by way of being born again, He has great plans lined up ahead for us. We certainly cannot consider ourselves the 'finished article' but more a 'work in progress'! He loves to encourage us into exploits that are more adventurous than we can possibly have imagined. Along the way He attempts to refine our characters using people and situations in order to produce a more Jesus-like result.

We are by no means exempt from the trials and troubles of the world; these also shape us. We can be lured by the 'terrorist' as much as the next man, but maybe we are quicker to see his schemes for what they are. We all fortunately have the benefit of knowing that we can prayerfully call on God for His help and protection.

In the Bible Jesus says, 'The thief [Satan] comes only to steal and kill and destroy; I have come that they may have life, and have it to the full' (John 10:10).

There is nothing in our lives that is hidden from God and no wrongdoing that is so great that it excludes us from His presence. He asks us to confess our sins and He will be faithful to forgive us and cleanse us from all unrighteousness (1 John 1:9).

Jesus said, 'I give them [My followers] eternal life, and they shall never perish; no one will snatch them out of My hand. My Father, who has given them to Me, is greater than all; no one can snatch them out of My Father's hand' (John 10:28–29).

I encourage you to seek God with all your heart. He will be found. This decision is the most important and vital decision you will ever make.

Now that I have finished writing this account I feel released, relieved and at peace. Life beckons . . .

MY HORSE FOR A KINGDOM

REFLECTIONS OF MY HEART

Poems written 1987–1988

PRAYER

I never thought the time would come
When I would kneel and pray,
And really take such pleasure in that time of day.
Did I want a Master?
I'd always been my own.
How I love the new life
My Lord that You have shown.
I gave my heart, I gave my soul,
I never knew such love,
What thankfulness I wished to give
To my Lord above.
And when I knew that I had found
The secret of the world,
I knew to die, would be to live
And bask in love unfurled.

COME FLY WITH ME

I lay awake as if on fire,
Beside me lay the man,
Who'd been my lover and my friend
Since our love began.

But, Lord, I yearned to be with You,
If only he could see,
And together find that peace and joy
And both of us be free.

He did not know and could not feel
Me slip away to you.
Please come with me, it's easy,
See. Just trust and meet Him too.

Lord, I didn't understand,
Forgive me my mistake,
I hoped that both of us could pass
Through that narrow gate.

I know one day you two will meet,
I long to see that day.
Smile kindly on him please, my Lord,
And help show him the way.

AWESOME GOD

To sink to my knees at your feet,
To rest with my head humbly bowed,
Your hand in mine, our hearts entwined,
How is it I'm here, I'm allowed?

You're the King of the whole universe,
Endless nations to care for and see,
How is it you've time? No waiting in line,
You never refuse to see me.

I'm learning to give You the reins,
I'm trusting in You more and more.
You know what I need, You planted the seed
I'm the one You gave your life for.

How terrific it is that we're friends,
My life is now Yours to command,
In all that I do, I have You there too,
Now life's troubled waters are calmed.

ABBA FATHER

To feel your heart soften, an ache that grows,
Eyes that prick, a tear that flows,
Knowing God's love just makes me complete
The safest of places, here at your feet.
A knowledge that worry's a thing of the past,
No longer alone. This friend will last.

Jesus, You watch like a father concerned,
Loving, encouraging, Your way confirmed.
How long do I wait till I'm there at Your throne?
I've gone through the door, but it's still far from home.
Time for You is a breath on the wind.
To us, the impatient, it's never to end.

Father, You're more than I dreamt You could be,
I marvel I found that one destiny.
I had no idea there was more to this life,
You'd given me all, no hunger or strife.
I didn't deserve, I still don't I know,
Now I've the chance my true love to show.

Thank You these lines can flow from my pen.
I'd love to give You the love of all men.
If only they'd listen and hark to Your call,
Your plan was a home in heaven for all.
So, chosen I am and pledged to You King
I give You my heart, my life, everything.

GRACE

*Did you ever wonder
What makes a new born child,
Have little bits of Mum and Dad
A masterpiece compiled?
He knew we'd be delighted
To see ourselves renewed,
That child. It's His, please do see that
So often we exclude.
That's grace you know!*

*Did you ever wonder
Why the seasons come and go.
From breath of spring to falling leaves
From daffodils to snow?
And every year another chance
To be dazzled by the sight,
It's just like life. Don't turn it down
Let in that God of light.
That's grace you know!*

*Did you ever wonder,
Have you ever lost a friend.
A person who had years ahead
Why did that life just end?
You knew it could be me or you,
Appreciate with praise,
Another chance to question life
Or Jesus name to raise.
That's grace you know!*

MY HORSE FOR A KINGDOM

Did you ever wonder
Why it's written down just so,
The way, the truth, life's formula
He wants us all to know?
How often Lord, You are ignored,
You mourn their coming death
They just can't say they never knew
You try till their last breath.
That's grace you know.

THE VISION – COMING IN BACKWARDS

At the back of that place.
Shining light and peace ahead.
What was I doing here? How beautiful.
What had I stumbled on?
Supposing I was noticed? I had no right to be here.
Yet I didn't want to turn around and go back to that blackness.
Quietly, Liz. Maybe no one will notice.
Don't speak, move calmly – so it went on.
The longer I stayed the more I knew I never wanted to leave.
This was everything I desired, completeness.
Then fear. Fear of being found out. Told to leave.
Don't disturb the status quo.
This place, so clear in my mind's eye.
Yet, how could it be?
Reassurance: I spoke, people were amazed,
Their love flowed out to me.
No mistake. I was welcome,
The door of the Kingdom of Heaven was open to me! To stay!
I wasn't a cheat, hadn't found a short cut.
I spoke things to the keeper of this place,
Come closer, My child, here, let Me see you clearly.
I want you to know Me because I love you so much
And have waited so long.

AND THEN

And then I had a friend,
I didn't know where He came from
Or who He was, except that we belonged together.
I'd never had a friend like this before.
We talked but there were no words.
When I called, He answered.
His reply hit my heart, wonderfully.
So many times in those first days,
Are You still there?
Relief, the heart of love replied.
Please don't go. Who are You?
And then I knew His name.
He wrote it on my soul.
Love and truth, and signed it God.
How could this possibly be? Not God
Not the one of Abraham and Isaac and now me!
But that one dealt with ancient nations,
This one dealt with me, personally!
But it was so. And it was forever.

Never will I leave you; never will I forsake you.
(Hebrews 13:5)